DEMYSTIFYING DIVERSITY

EMBRACING OUR SHARED HUMANITY

WORKBOOK

Daralyse Lyons

Loving Healing Press

Ann Arbor, MI

To connect with the author directly, or to learn more, please visit www.daralyselyons.com or www.demystifyingdiversitypodcast.com.

ISBN 978-1-61599-536-3

Published by
Loving Healing Press
5145 Pontiac Trail
Ann Arbor, MI 48105

www.LHPress.com   Tollfree 888-761-6268
info@LHPress.com   Fax 734-663-6861

Contents

Introduction

If you have purchased a copy of the *Demystifying Diversity Workbook*, I commend you. It's one thing to feel for those we believe to be different than ourselves; it's another to actively grapple with our biases and be willing to move beyond them. Yet, it is in this space that empathy and equity become possible. If you find yourself looking at the world—and wishing things could be better—know that real change begins with us. It starts with people like you and me and the wonderful individuals who contributed their wisdom and insights to the Demystifying Diversity project. It starts by acknowledging the problems and empowering ourselves and our communities to take an active role in the solution.

The results of oppression are all too evident. Systemic change is necessary. But, since individuals comprise and participate in systems, until more of us expand our capacity for empathy, things can't get better. I don't mean to be pessimistic. In fact, I have the utmost confidence in human beings. When we love one another, all things are possible. The problem is that we don't do a very good job of loving one another because of our learned discrimination and dehumanization. This workbook is meant to teach you how to love yourself and others, or, at the very least, behave with kindness and compassion in the hope that your heart will shift with the continued application of new actions and ideas.

This workbook is meant to act as a companion to the book *Demystifying Diversity: Embracing Our Shared Humanity*. I would encourage you to work through the book and the workbook simultaneously, stopping at the end of each chapter to do the corresponding workbook exercises before returning to your reading. However, if you want to utilize this workbook without reading the accompanying book, that is fine. You won't gain a larger context, but it's far better to apply the principles of love and connection than not to do so.

You can engage with this workbook and its exercises on your own or with others, as part of a book group or with a friend or family member. It can be a wonderfully enriching experience to share your process as you move forward. Again, I admire your courage and I know that this workbook will be incredibly beneficial for you and for others. Join me on this journey to demystify diversity and to find the shared humanity that exists within all of us.

You can engage with this workbook and its exercises on your own or with others, as part of a book group or with a friend or family member. If you are a training facilitator, or if you are considering utilizing this workbook as part of a corporate diversity initiative, see the appendix for helpful tips on how to utilize this workbook with a group. It can be a wonderfully enriching experience to share your process as you move forward. Again, I admire your courage and I know that this workbook will be incredibly beneficial for you and for others. Join me on this journey to demystify diversity and to find the shared humanity that exists within all of us.

Disclaimer

When it comes to expanding the scope of our understanding of diversity, equity and inclusion, it is important to be willing to step outside our respective and constrictive comfort zones. That said, this workbook and the book it is based upon invites you to engage in a meaningful way with experiences and outlooks with which you may lack familiarity. If you arrive at a section of a chapter that discusses information with which you have firsthand experience, or if you are a member of a marginalized group, please do what is in keeping with your need for safety and self-preservation. If a section does not apply to you, skip it or modify in such a way as to support your growth and ensure your emotional safety.

Exercises for Preface

Exercise P-1: In the space provided below, answer the following questions: What's the reason you bought this book? If someone else bought it for you, why did they? Did you discuss their reasoning? How did that conversation make you feel?

_____

_____

_____

_____

_____

Exercise P-2: What do you think would change about your life if you learned about people whose identity markers include cultures, religions, races, sexual orientations, body shapes, and physical and/or cognitive abilities other than your own?

_____

_____

_____

_____

Exercise P-3: What do you want people to know about you that they generally wouldn't realize based on your visible or invisible identity markers?

_____

_____

_____

_____

Exercise P-4: Take the Diversity Pledge

If you can honestly agree to the following pledge, sign and date below.

Diversity Pledge

In signing this, I own and acknowledge that I have been part of the problem of pervasive othering that is occurring within the world. I have made judgments about people I did not know based on my own faulty assumptions. I cannot promise to let go of all my prejudice, privilege and/or self-important superiority, but I can and will keep an open mind as I move forward on this journey of growth and exploration. It is only by accepting that I have been part of the problem that I can become part of the solution.

Signed_____

Date_____

Exercises for Chapter 1 – Diversity and Me: Early Experiences

Exercise 1-1: It has been said that the eyes are a window into the soul, yet we don't often make eye-contact with others. We almost never look into our own eyes longer than it takes us to remove a wayward lash or put on mascara. For the next week, spend two full minutes every day staring into your own eyes in the mirror. Connect with the parts of yourself that go deeper than your external appearance, deeper than what you think you know about who you are. Really look. Become curious. Mark one square for each day you do the exercise: □ □ □ □ □ □ □

At the end of the week, answer the following questions:

A) What did you notice from doing the mirror exercise each day?

_____

_____

_____

_____

B) Did anything surprise you about the process or about yourself?

_____

_____

_____

_____

C) What do you see when you attempt to see your soul?

_____

_____

_____

_____

_____

D) What are your major takeaways?

_____

_____

_____

_____

Exercise 1-2: Over the course of the next week, strike up a conversation with at least three people whose external appearance makes you think *I don't have anything in common with this person.* For this exercise, it's not enough to simply say hello. Talk to each person until you discover at least one similarity that feels significant to you. If you walk away without identifying something about them that reminds you of yourself, the encounter doesn't count. Keep going until you've found a way to relate to three, seemingly "unlike you" individuals from a place of sameness, rather than of difference. Mark one square for each day you do it: ☐ ☐ ☐ ☐ ☐ ☐ ☐

At the end of the week, answer the following questions:

A) What did you notice about meeting each person?

_____

_____

_____

_____

B) What did you have in common with each person?

_____

_____

_____

_____

C) How did these interactions challenge your initial perceptions?

_____

_____

_____

_____

D) What lessons have you learned about the way you see other people?

_____

_____

_____

_____

E) How can you grow as a result of these encounters?

_____

_____

_____

_____

Exercises for Chapter 2 – Encountering the Black/White Binary

Exercise 2-1: You may have noticed that, throughout this book, I have capitalized race – White, Black, Biracial, etc. This is because racial and ethnic groups have been designated proper nouns. We've been taught that language, particularly English, is stagnant when the opposite is far more true. Language has shifted and will continue to shift over time. Stepping away from binaries means becoming more comfortable with the flexibility (and constant evolution) of words, terms, and phrases. Race has not always been capitalized.

A) Were you aware of this shift in word usage and capitalization? How do you feel about this?

_____

_____

_____

_____

B) What do you think of the fact that the rules of language shift regarding race?

_____

_____

_____

_____

C) Write about the emotional impact of language fluidity and whether or not you experience an emotional reaction to the changes in language, capitalization, and terminology.

_____

_____

_____

_____

Exercise 2-2: Most of us have experienced what can be described as "racial moments" in our lifetimes. These can include a whole host of experiences and interactions having to do with race. Think about your past and identify a moment from your life where race became a central point, ideally a moment in which you felt a level of discomfort.

A) Write about the experience and what about it made you feel unsettled.

_____

_____

_____

_____

_____

B) What, if anything, did you learn from this experience?

_____

_____

_____

_____

C) How has it changed you?

_____

_____

_____

_____

D) Does it continue to impact your understanding of race?

_____

_____

_____

Exercises for Chapter 3 – What Biracial Identity Can Teach Us

Exercise 3-1: Until you love and accept your racial and ethnic backgrounds, even if they're problematized by history, prejudice, difficulty, or privilege, you won't be able to fully embrace all races.

A) As part of the process of embracing the up- and down-sides of your ancestral legacy, make a list of all the ethnicities that comprise you

_____

_____

_____

_____

B) List at least ten things that you can embrace about each of them.

1. _____

2. _____

3. _____

4. _____

5. _____

6. _____

7. _____ \

8. _____

9. _____

10. _____

C) Write down five possible sources of shame associated with each ethnicity. If you can't think of at least fifteen things to list, research your various cultures until you can.

1. _____

2. _____

3. _____

4. _____

5. _____

6. _____

7. _____ \

8. _____

9. _____

10. _____

11. _____

12. _____

13. _____

14. _____

15. _____

D) Study your lists and let yourself acknowledge the complexity of your history. Then, journal about how you feel and what you can personally do to move away from the sources of shame into the sources of strength.

_____

_____

_____

_____

_____

_____

Exercise 3-2: Identify at least three people with diverse racial or ethnic backgrounds (by which I mean they are multiethnic or Biracial) with which you have close relationships

A) People in my life with multi-ethnic or Biracial backgrounds

_____   _____

_____   _____

_____   _____

_____   _____

B) Reach out to ask them if they're open to speaking about their spectrum experiences of race and ethnicity. These conversations should be voice to voice in person, on the phone, or through video chat so you can connect and focus without distraction. Journal about what you've learned.

_____

_____

_____

_____

_____

_____

_____

C) If you don't have at least three people in your life who are multiethnic or Biracial, ask yourself Why not? Then, journal about any insights that arise.

_____

_____

_____

_____

_____

_____

Exercises for Chapter 4 – No More Bystanders

Exercise 4-1: Think about an incident where you witnessed someone being cruel or hurtful to another human being and opted not to intervene. Recall the experience as vividly as possible.

A) **Where were you?**

_____

_____

B) **What were you thinking and feeling?**

_____

_____

_____

_____

C) **Was there a moment when you thought about intervening? If so, what stopped you? Journal about your emotions and reflections.**

_____

_____

_____

_____

_____

_____

_____

_____

D) Envision being in the same situation again and imagine what you might have done differently. See yourself taking constructive action. Journal about what you'd have done, if you could rewrite history, and how it would have made you feel to get involved instead of remaining on the sidelines.

_____

_____

_____

_____

_____

_____

_____

_____

_____

E) If you are able to, and it would not hurt the person, contact the victim and apologize for the part you played in allowing their perpetrator to harm them. If you are not able to do that, write an apology letter in the space provided below. Don't send the letter, but, when you're done writing, read it aloud to yourself.

_____

_____

_____

_____

_____

_____

_____

F) If it is safe, contact the perpetrator separately and tell them how their behavior hurt you and why, if you could go back now, you'd have stood up to them. If that is not a viable option, write a letter to the perpetrator, then read that letter aloud to yourself.

_____

_____

_____

_____

_____

G) If you were ever harmed and there was a witness to that harm, write a letter to that person letting them know how their lack of intercession hurt you.

_____

_____

_____

_____

_____

Exercises for Chapter 5 – Unconditional Love

Exercise 5-1: List all the people in your life that you genuinely and profoundly love. Beside each person, list all the instances in which you have failed to exhibit unconditional love towards them. I'm not talking about the times you overreacted or yelled or displayed less than your best self. This isn't an audit on your capacity to exhibit relational perfection. Instead, you're listing the times when you either explicitly or implicitly conveyed the message that there was something "wrong" with them.

_____

_____

_____

_____

_____

_____

_____

_____

_____

Exercise 5-2: Write each of these individuals a letter letting them know where and how you were wrong and, if they're still in your life, spelling out the ways in which you plan to be different moving forward. Don't give any of the people on your list the letter, or promise them you'll change. To do those things would be to make your inability to be the person they deserve about you, and love requires us to put the other person first.

_____

_____

_____

_____

_____

_____

_____

_____

_____

_____

_____

Exercise 5-3: Commit to practicing the actions of affection towards this person (or people) every day for the next 30 days. Once you've been able to exhibit unconditional love for 30 continuous days, then you can apologize for your previous failings. If you can't make 30 continuous days, start your day count over after every slip. Do so without shame. Just resolve to learn from your mistakes and more forward differently. Love yourself enough to be an imperfect, ever-evolving human. The more you practice love, the more your relationships will improve, and the quality of our lives is determined by the quality of our relationships.

Write down the date of each day you expressed unconditional love below

_____   _____   _____   _____   _____   _____

_____   _____   _____   _____   _____   _____

_____   _____   _____   _____   _____   _____

_____   _____   _____   _____   _____   _____

_____   _____   _____   _____   _____   _____

Exercises for Chapter 6 – Practice Being Anti-Racist

Exercise 6-1: Think about a racial incident that occurred in your life. Write all the steps involved. For an example, see page 52 in this chapter where I catalogue the progression of moments and choices that occurred between Amy Cooper and Christian Cooper in Central Park. Beside each step, rank how well you lived up to your own personal values using a scale of zero to ten (zero being not at all, ten being completely). If you ranked each step a ten, find a different incident. The point is not to assess your relative "wokeness" but to identify opportunities for growth. For every step that you did not rank a ten, ask yourself:

Ranking   **What Happened?**

_____   _____

                 _____

                 _____

_____   _____

                 _____

_____   _____

                 _____

_____   _____

_____

_____

_____   _____

_____

_____

B) What could you have done differently that would have been in keeping with your values and beliefs? The purpose of this process is not to get you to mentally berate yourself but, rather, for you to find moments of interruption, moments in which you can rehearse and rewire your cultural conditioning. Once you've determined a course of action that would have been your ideal scenario for how you'd have opted to behave, write the story of that experience as if you'd conducted yourself as your highest, most authentic, you.

_____

_____

_____

_____

_____

Exercise 6-2: We all have biases and, until we can own up to them, we're only perpetuating the problem.

A) Identify one or more racial or ethnic groups against which you hold one or more biases. Be honest.

_____

_____

_____

_____

_____

_____

B) Select the group against which you feel the greatest resistance, fear, judgment, or prejudice. Over the next week, arrange to connect with members of that racial or ethnic group in a meaningful, interpersonal way. For example, you could volunteer for an organization that has a direct, positive impact on the lives of members of the racial or ethnic group against which you hold a bias, schedule a trip to the country of origin of those individuals and get to know local inhabitants, or meet with a priest, pastor, rabbi, or Imam who ministers to members of that community and ask them for recommendations for spiritual acts of service that you can do to become a better ally. The possibilities are endless. Whatever you opt to do, make sure that it's meaningful, interactive, and connected. One of the best things we can do to promote greater diversity and inclusion is to interact with individuals who, at first glance, might appear to be different than ourselves. Step outside your comfort zone and you'll learn that you've been living in a self-imposed (and societally-imposed) prison cell. Use the space on the next page to describe what confronted you the most as well as what unexpected pleasure you got out of doing it.

_____

_____

_____

Exercises for Chapter 7 – Agency

Exercise 7-1: Let's explore the people in your life who may have any type of disability, including physical or mental. Be sure to consider those who may have invisible disabilities.

A) Do you have any people with disabilities in your life? List them below

_____   _____

_____   _____

_____   _____

B) If so, how do you treat these individuals? Is your way of loving them empowering or disempowering?

_____

_____

_____

_____

_____

C) How much are you supporting their individual agency?

_____

_____

_____

_____

_____

D) Where are you pushing your own agenda without regard to these people's thoughts, feelings and interests?

_____

_____

_____

_____

_____

E) If you do not have any individuals with disabilities in your immediate circle, is there anyone in your life for whom you are making decisions, without regard to their wants and desires (even if you tell yourself it's in their best interests)? Journal about the relationships in which you are in a position where you could play an active part in supporting someone's self-advocacy.

_____

_____

_____

_____

_____

F) Where have you been negligent? When have you been judgmental? What could you do to be a better ally?

_____

_____

_____

_____

_____

Exercise 7-2: Let's explore how you have interacted casually with people who have disabilities throughout your entire lifetime. As with Exercise 7-1, please consider those with either physical or mental disabilities.

A) Have you ever made fun of someone based on your perception of their differences? If so, what did you tell yourself about that person, or those people, when you were devaluing and/or dehumanizing them?

_____

_____

_____

_____

_____

_____

B) Did you do it to their face or behind their back?

_____

_____

_____

C) What actions have you taken to make amends? If you haven't made things right, determine a strategy for doing so. This is best done by making direct amends, but, if that's not possible, come up with a meaningful alternative. Find a way to directly engage with those you have seen as other. Before you do so, however, internalize the following reality: the gift of the interaction will not be your presence in their lives. It will be their presence in yours.

_____

_____

_____

_____

_____

_____

_____

_____

_____

_____

Exercises for Chapter 8 – Belonging, Inclusivity, and Culture

Exercise 8-1: If you've never interacted with a Muslim person and don't know anything about the faith, this is the beginning of the end of ignorance. There are a number of ways that you can educate yourself. The first step is to find a reputable source that was created for beginners seeking to learn more. Some options might be to sign up for a course, purchase a book, download an audiobook, or even subscribe to a podcast.

A) List your action plan steps below for powering up your knowledge of Muslims and their practice of faith. As you complete each one, mark the checkbox to signify it's done.

☐ _____

☐ _____

☐ _____

☐ _____

☐ _____

☐ _____

☐ _____

☐ _____

☐ _____

Exercise 8-2: Over the next month, spend at least 15 minutes every day engaging with new information and expanding your perspective. As you increase your exposure, focus on the principles, beliefs, and thoughts that resonate with you. This isn't about wholehearted subscription to the faith but learning more about a rich spiritual tradition that has a lot to offer to Muslims and non-Muslims alike. Mark a checkbox each day that you engage in learning:

Week 1 ☐☐☐☐☐☐☐   Week 2 ☐☐☐☐☐☐☐
Week 3 ☐☐☐☐☐☐☐   Week 4 ☐☐☐☐☐☐☐

A) List or journal about principles, beliefs, and thoughts of the Islamic faith as you discover them. It's ok to disagree, the point is that you learn something new.

Exercise 8-3: Go to www.cair.com/get-involved/become-an-ally/ and take three of the concrete actions listed on the site to become an ally.

A) The three actions I am taking to become an ally are:

1. _____

_____

_____

_____

2. _____

_____

_____

_____

3. _____

_____

_____

_____

Exercises for Chapter 9 – Appreciate, Don't Appropriate

Exercise 9-1: There are so many incredible inventions and innovations to come out of Asian cultures—from the pocket-calculator (Japan) to the Galaxy Smartphone (Korea) to the Automated Teller Machine (Vietnam)—but because of all of the post-COVID-19 anti-Chinese sentiment, I have chosen to focus on China. In this exercise, I challenge you to go an entire day without using any of the following ten inventions, or any of their derivatives, all of which are Chinese innovations.

1. Umbrella
2. Abacus – this means no computer, since the abacus was a precursor to the modern-day computer.
3. Compass – since compasses are used to provide directions, this means no GPS or navigation systems.
4. Gunpowder and/or Fireworks
5. Porcelain
6. Paper – this includes writing paper, toilet paper, paper money, and all other paper products.
7. Silk
8. Noodles
9. Tooth Brush
10. Seismograph

If you've gotten to the end of this list, you'll have realized that a day without these ten items would be nearly impossible. Even if you could refrain from using your computer, or your GPS, it would be untenable to go without toilet paper or a toothbrush. Breathe a sigh of relief. You don't have to go a day without using all of the above, but I would ask you to imagine what it would be like to forgo these essential innovations. Choose five inventions from this list of ten that have the most tangible benefit to your life.

A) Journal about the various ways in which each of 5 selected innovations enriches your world.

1. _____

_____

_____

2. _____

_____

_____

3. _____

_____

_____

4. _____

_____

_____

5, _____

_____

Exercise 9-2: Identify an Asian culture in which you can take an active interest. Commit to learning more about some element of that culture. For example, you can sign up for a sushi-making or watercolor-painting class (Japan), enroll in a Mandarin language course (China), or read a book about the history of Vietnam. Don't stop at the surface. Explore the underlying philosophy and/or motivation behind your selected area of inquiry. Appreciate the value that comes from engaging with another culture.

A) The Asian culture(s) which I choose to explore is/are:

_____

_____

B) Cultural areas of interest I will consider studying are:

1. _____

_____

_____

2. _____

_____

_____

3. _____

_____

_____

Exercise 9-3: Since we don't often practice engaged listening, for the next week, that will be your aim. Engage in one conversation every day during which your aim is to hear the other person, rather than to be heard. For each of these seven conversations, pay 100% attention, 100% of the time. Do not multitask. Focus on the person in front of you, or on the phone, and listen intently. After each conversation, write down what you noticed and how active listening impacted the quality of your interaction.

Sunday_____

_____

_____

_____

Monday_____

_____

_____

_____

Tuesday_____

_____

_____

_____

Wednesday_____

_____

_____

_____

Thursday_____

_____

_____

_____

Friday_____

_____

_____

Saturday_____

_____

_____

Exercises for Chapter 10 – Embodiment

Exercise 10-1: Write down all your current food rules.

A) What won't you allow yourself to eat? What do you tell yourself is off-limits?

_____

_____

_____

_____

B) What, if any, time parameters or location parameters or exercise rules have you set for yourself?

_____

_____

_____

_____

C) Then, go through each and every rule, and beside it, write down your reason for the rule. Where did it come from? Is it your rule or someone else's? What does adherence to it offer you? What does it cost you?

_____

_____

_____

_____

_____

_____

_____

_____

_____

_____

Exercise 10-2: How do you feel about your body?

A) Write down everything you think about your appearance.

_____

_____

_____

_____

_____

B) What do you like about your body?

_____

_____

_____

_____

C) What do you dislike?

_____

_____

_____

_____

_____

Exercise 10-3: How do you feel inside your body? Write about the internal experience of being in your body. Notice physical sensations, emotions, and anything else that you experience. If you aren't able to access an internal experience of feeling embodied, write about that. Simply become present to what is.

_____

_____

_____

_____

_____

_____

_____

_____

Exercise 10-4: Is your relationship with food neutral? If not, what gets in the way of you feeling balanced around food, body and weight?

_____

_____

_____

_____

_____

_____

_____

_____

_____

Exercise 10-5: For the next three days, any time you hear a comment about food, weight, body, exercise, etc. —anything that might be codified as part of the rhetoric or the rules of diet culture—mark an "X" in the box. At the end of the three days, count how many times you overheard or said something that is part of diet culture. Reflect on how many messages you heard or participated in and journal about what this number means to you.

Day 1: □
□ □ □ □ □ □ □ □ □ □ □ □ □ □ □ □ □ □ □ □
□ □ □ □ □ □ □ □ □ □ □ □ □ □ □ □ □ □ □ □
□ □ □ □ □ □ □ □ □ □ □ □ □ □ □ □ □ □ □ □
□ □ □ □ □ □ □ □ □ □ □ □ □ □ □ □ □ □ □ □

Day 2: □
□ □ □ □ □ □ □ □ □ □ □ □ □ □ □ □ □ □ □ □
□ □ □ □ □ □ □ □ □ □ □ □ □ □ □ □ □ □ □ □
□ □ □ □ □ □ □ □ □ □ □ □ □ □ □ □ □ □ □ □
□ □ □ □ □ □ □ □ □ □ □ □ □ □ □ □ □ □ □ □

Day 3: □
□ □ □ □ □ □ □ □ □ □ □ □ □ □ □ □ □ □ □ □
□ □ □ □ □ □ □ □ □ □ □ □ □ □ □ □ □ □ □ □
□ □ □ □ □ □ □ □ □ □ □ □ □ □ □ □ □ □ □ □
□ □ □ □ □ □ □ □ □ □ □ □ □ □ □ □ □ □ □ □

Exercise 10-6: Identify one "rule" or belief of diet culture that you will commit to being an advocate against and make a personal resolution to fight against this rule within yourself and within the world. For example, if you decide that you will reject weight, throw out your scale and refuse to talk about weight with friends and family. If you've been doing Paleo and decide to stop vilifying carbs, allow yourself to incorporate new foods, ditch the diet cookbooks, and on family dinner nights, instead of sticking to salads, incorporate a wider repertoire. You don't have to start with something big. Simply choose something you can commit to, something that will help you find freedom in yourself and in the world,

A) I commit to being an advocate against this rule or belief of diet culture

_____

_____

_____

_____

_____

Exercises for Chapter 11 – Coming Out of the Shadows through Community

Exercise 11-1: Make a list of all the skills you possess that can contribute something to the lives of others. This isn't a time to be modest. List every skill you can identify as well as those that others have recognized within you.

_____

_____

_____

_____

Exercise 11-2: Make a list of all the communities and groups of which you are a part.

_____

_____

_____

_____

Exercise 11-3: Looking over the two lists you've created, decide which communities you want to contribute to over the next two weeks and which skills you can utilize to do so. Write a list of ten actions that you can take that will contribute to your various communities. Over the next two weeks, do every item on the list. (If one of the actions requires a longer, more involved process, at the very least, make a start on every item).

1. _____

_____

2. _____

_____

3. _____

_____

4. _____

_____

5. _____

_____

6. _____

_____

7. _____

8. _____

_____

9. _____

_____

10. _____

_____

Exercise 11-4: Immigrants have contributed so much to this nation and, no doubt, to your life. Find an organization that is doing good work to encourage the upward social mobility of those who are benefitting your life and find a way to give back to that community in a way that actually requires an investment. Give time, give money, give resources, give whatever will feel significant and do so from a place of gratitude knowing that the path to success is never a purely individual endeavor. Contribute to the good of others from your recognition that you have something to offer and that they do, too.

I commit to contributing resources that I can to this immigrant support organization(s)

_____

_____

Exercise 11-5: Over the next week, discover a person, an organization, or a resource that you can teach something to and learn something from in return. Have a moment of authentic and mutual learning wherein you are both teacher and student. These types of interactions go a long way toward teaching us the value of horizontal, as opposed to hierarchal, learning. Write about what you were able to learn or teach.

_____

_____

_____

_____

_____

_____

_____

_____

Exercises for Chapter 12 – Running Together

Exercise 12-1: Think about all the rules and beliefs that you have about your race and culture.

A) What do you tell yourself about who you are and how you ought to behave?

_____

_____

_____

_____

B) Where did these rules come from? Are they things you learned based on what you were told? What you experienced?

_____

_____

_____

_____

C) Make a list of all the things you tell yourself you have to do because of your race and/or culture.

_____

_____

_____

_____

D) Make a list of all the things you tell yourself you can't do because of your race or culture.

_____

_____

_____

_____

E) Identify a rule that does not originate from your own internal values and makes you feel a sense of internal hypocrisy. Invite yourself to break that rule.

_____

_____

_____

Exercise 12-2: Identify something about your culture or upbringing that means a lot to you—a tradition, a meal, a practice, etc. —and share this important element of yourself with someone in your inner circle. Tell them about it, invite them to participate, and stretch beyond your prior boundaries. Write about the reactions that people had to you telling them about it. Did they already know? Were they surprised or inspired by anything?

_____

_____

_____

_____

_____

_____

_____

Exercises for Chapter 13 – Putting the Glass Back Together

Exercise 13-1: On page 2 of this workbook, you signed a diversity pledge. Go back and read that again.

A) List some ways in which you were able to fulfill the pledge

_____

_____

_____

_____

B) List some ways in which you failed to fulfill the intent of the pledge

_____

_____

_____

_____

Exercise 13-2: As you look back on your journey to Demystify Diversity and all the inner evolution that's occurred, as well as how your capacity to engage with others has shifted, write the story of your future if you were to conduct your actions and interactions free of all biases and to connect with others across a broad spectrum of humanity.

What could the future be if all the limits you've placed on your ability to love (or that have been taught to you by others) were to fall away and you could simply be a human being?

_____

_____

_____

_____

_____

_____

_____

_____

_____

Exercise 13-3: If you haven't yet connected with a community, your mission for the next week is to find a community that you can join. You might find a volunteer organization, a mutual aid network, a tenant's association, an artists' collective, a personal development community (like the Next Level Community, of which I am an active and engaged member), or an improv comedy group (I'm a company member with ComedySportz and that's been so supportive and fun!). The possibilities are endless. The point is: Find people that matter to you and to whom you will matter and commit to building together, growing together, and liberating one another.

A) I commit to joining the following community

_____

_____

And please know that the *Demystifying Diversity Podcast* is also creating our own community, of which you are a part. Find us at www.demystifyingdiversitypodcast.com and send us messages, leave us voicemails, connect with us on social media, join our events, and surround yourself with people who want to know and love you exactly as you are.

Appendix – Information for Groups and Organizations Looking to Utilize the *Demystifying Diversity Workbook*

If you have decided to use the *Demystifying Diversity Workbook* as part of a group initiative, such as in a nonprofit organization or in a corporate setting, it's important to move through the book, *Demystifying Diversity: Embracing our Shared Humanity* and workbook in tandem. Ideally, you'd read each chapter of the book and discuss that chapter, then progress to the corresponding section in the workbook, reflecting on each exercise after you have completed it before moving on to the next chapter in *Demystifying Diversity: Embracing our Shared Humanity*. Since every organization has its own unique culture, I encourage you to find a structure and a schedule that will be effective for your particular group. As you create a plan, I encourage you to keep the following suggestions in mind:

1. Navigate this process in a timely manner. You'll want to give participants the opportunity to read through and engage with the material without rushing or lagging behind. *Demystifying Diversity: Embracing our Shared Humanity* contains a foreword, a preface and 13 chapters, and the *Demystifying Diversity Workbook* is comprised of an introduction, followed by exercises for the preface and each of the 13 chapters. I'd suggest moving through the book and its accompanying workbook by meeting weekly or bi-weekly to discuss a book chapter and its corresponding workbook section or, if you would prefer, to alternate between discussing the written chapters and the corresponding workbook assignments.

2. Accountability can be helpful. If your organization is committed to doing this work, ask employees to commit to working through the book and workbook in their entirety. It can be supportive to assign partners or to create interim quizzes. No one should be made to feel like this is a chore, but the higher the rate of participation, the better your outcomes will be – both within your organization and with the world.

3. Promise confidentiality and safety. Diversity and inclusion work is most effective when people feel free to share in a safe environment, trusting that their words will not be weaponized against them. Make it clear that people should feel free to share their thoughts and feelings, that anything said within the safety of a group session will be kept confidential and that employees are expected to respect one another's privacy.

4. Consider the power dynamics of your organization and try not to replicate those within the learning environment. It may seem obvious that we have a tendency to share differently with those we perceive to be our peers than with those who have more or less authority than we do. As you are designing your sessions, think critically about how to bring equity to the space. The more equal and inclusive this work can be, the better the outcomes. Liberation requires dispensing with hierarchal or oppressive structures.

5. Make it fun. Laughter is healing! This might be serious stuff, but we don't have to take ourselves too seriously. Encourage whoever is facilitating the group discussions to find opportunities for levity and to be willing to share their own imperfect moments.

6. Talk about how and where participants see applications for this work within your organization. Encourage individuals to voice their ideas and to find ways of applying the lessons from the book and workbook to their everyday experiences in the office or organization. Ask one another: How can we create a better, more uplifting environment for ourselves and a more inviting place for others? Theory is great; however, it's only by putting theory into practice that we begin to see positive and productive shifts.

7. Engage with the larger community, beyond your organization. How can you take in-class, or in-office, learning out into the world in a meaningful way? What's a project your organization can become inspired to do that fits the principles of diversity, equity and inclusion? The possibilities are endless. Challenge your group to dream together, and let everyone play a role in devising a project that will improve the community and, by extension, the world.

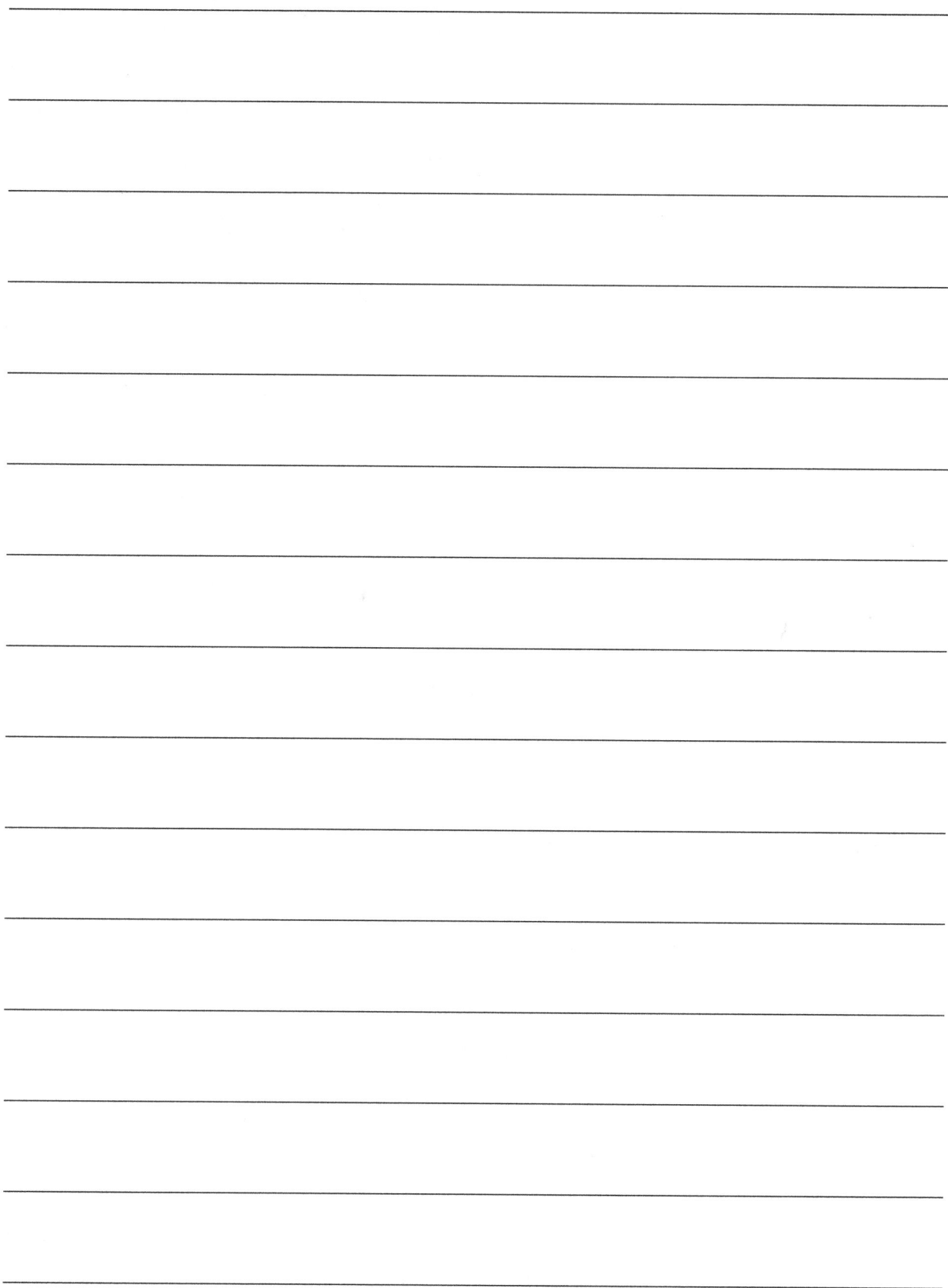

This workbook is designed to be used in conjunction with
Demystifying Diversity: Embracing Our Shared Humanity

It can be difficult to find reliable information that amplifies the voices and the viewpoints of those who have direct experience dealing with diversity, equity and inclusion. In *Demystifying Diversity: Embracing our Shared Humanity*, Biracial journalist Daralyse Lyons has interviewed more than 100 individuals—academics, politicians, thought-leaders, advocates, activists and even an incarcerated inmate—and reveals her most important information and insights. By engaging with this text, you will find areas of human intersection and connection that challenge your biases and break down your barriers. Through empathy and understanding, we can create a more inclusive world.

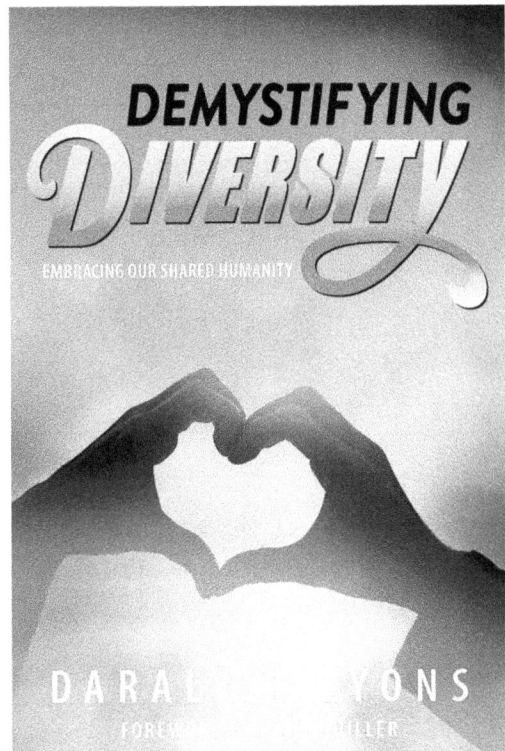

"The work of any reconciliation along the lines of the basis of identity requires vulnerability, a vulnerability that we are told is not of value to the American way of being."
 -- Paul Reese, Master of Divinity, Yale Divinity School

"Exposure and practice prepare people for unpredictable racial moments."
 -- Dr. Howard Stevenson, director, Racial Empowerment Collaborative

"We are siblings in humanity. No one has superiority over another, except by their character."
-- Nihad Awad, executive director and co-founder of the Council on American-Islamic Relations

"In the present—and correcting the ills of the past—our public policy needs to always move towards equity. If we can do that, I think, as a society, we're going to get better."
 -- Senator Sharif Street, third senatorial district of Philadelphia

Learn more about the Demystifying Diversity project and podcast at DemystifyingDiversityPodcast.com and connect with the author at DaralyseLyons.com

ISBN 978-1-61599-533-2

paperback * hardcover * eBook

www.LHPress.com

Write to info@LHPress.com for information about quantity discounts for any of our book products.

www.ingramcontent.com/pod-product-compliance
Lightning Source LLC
Chambersburg PA
CBHW080055280326
41934CB00014B/3320